The Reagan Era

American history, Volume 14

Michael Johnson

Published by Harmony House Publishing, 2024.

THE REAGAN ERA

First edition. April 5, 2024.

Copyright © 2024 Michael Johnson.

ISBN: 979-8224697717

Written by Michael Johnson.

Table of Contents

"To those who lived through the tumultuous and transformative Reagan era,

This book is dedicated to the individuals who witnessed firsthand the seismic shifts in American politics, society, and culture during the Reagan administration. To the activists, scholars, and citizens who engaged in spirited debates and shaped the course of our nation's history. Your resilience, passion, and commitment to democratic ideals inspire us to reflect on the complexities of the past and navigate the challenges of the present with wisdom and courage.

With deepest gratitude and respect,

Michael Johnson"

Chapter I: Introduction

A. Setting the Stage: America in the Late 20th Century

The late 20th century was a time of significant social, political, and economic change in America. Emerging from the turmoil of the 1960s, the nation faced a myriad of challenges, including economic stagflation, social unrest, and a crisis of confidence in government institutions. The Vietnam War had deeply divided the country, leading to widespread protests and a loss of trust in political leadership. The Watergate scandal further eroded faith in the integrity of government, culminating in the resignation of President Richard Nixon in 1974.

By the late 1970s, America found itself in a state of malaise, grappling with high inflation, rising unemployment, and declining international prestige. The energy crisis of 1973 had exposed the nation's vulnerability to external shocks, while the Iranian Revolution of 1979 and subsequent hostage crisis underscored the challenges of maintaining stability in a rapidly changing world. Against this backdrop of uncertainty and disillusionment, a new political movement began to emerge—one that would come to define the era: conservatism.

B. Rise of Conservatism: Pre-Reagan Era

The roots of the conservative movement in America can be traced back to the post-World War II era, with the rise of figures such as Barry Goldwater and William F. Buckley Jr. Goldwater's 1964 presidential campaign, though unsuccessful, galvanized a growing coalition of grassroots activists, intellectuals, and disillusioned Democrats who sought to push back against the perceived excesses of liberalism.

Throughout the 1970s, conservative thinkers and activists worked tirelessly to build a cohesive ideological framework grounded in principles of limited government, free markets, and traditional values. Organizations like the Heritage Foundation and the American Conservative Union provided intellectual firepower and grassroots organizing support, while media outlets such as

National Review and talk radio hosts like Rush Limbaugh helped to amplify conservative voices and shape public opinion.

By the late 1970s, the conservative movement had gained significant momentum, culminating in the election of Ronald Reagan as President in 1980. Reagan's victory marked the beginning of a new era in American politics—one characterized by a renewed emphasis on individual liberty, free enterprise, and a robust national defense.

C. Reagan's Ascendancy: Political Landscape and Personal Background

Ronald Reagan's journey to the White House was unlike that of any other modern president. Born in 1911 in rural Illinois, Reagan came of age during the Great Depression, witnessing firsthand the devastating impact of economic hardship on his family and community. After graduating from Eureka College, Reagan embarked on a career in entertainment, first as a radio announcer and later as a Hollywood actor.

Reagan's years in Hollywood provided him with a platform to hone his communication skills and develop a knack for connecting with audiences. Despite his success in show business, Reagan harbored political ambitions from an early age, eventually transitioning to a career in public service.

Reagan's political journey began in earnest in the 1960s, when he emerged as a vocal critic of big government and excessive taxation. As governor of California from 1967 to 1975, Reagan implemented a conservative agenda focused on tax cuts, deregulation, and law and order. His confrontations with student protesters and his tough stance on crime earned him the admiration of conservatives nationwide, paving the way for his eventual run for the presidency.

By the late 1970s, Reagan had become the standard-bearer of the conservative movement, espousing a vision of America as a shining city on a hill—a beacon of freedom and opportunity for all. His optimism and charisma resonated with voters disillusioned by years of economic stagnation and foreign policy setbacks, propelling him to victory in the 1980 presidential election.

As Reagan prepared to assume office, the political landscape of America stood at a crossroads. The liberal consensus that had dominated American politics for decades was beginning to crumble, replaced by a newfound sense of confidence and optimism among conservatives. With Reagan at the helm, the stage was set for a conservative revolution—one that would reshape the course of American history for years to come.

Chapter II: The Road to the White House

Ronald Reagan's journey to the White House was a remarkable odyssey that spanned decades and transformed the landscape of American politics. From his humble beginnings in the Midwest to his rise as the standard-bearer of the conservative movement, Reagan's path to power was marked by perseverance, charisma, and a steadfast commitment to his principles. In this chapter, we will explore the key milestones of Reagan's political career, from his early days as a Hollywood actor to his historic victories in the presidential campaigns of 1980 and 1984. We will also delve into Reagan's vision for America—a vision grounded in the principles of conservatism and focused on revitalizing the nation's economy, restoring its strength on the world stage, and reaffirming its commitment to individual liberty and traditional values.

A. Early Political Career of Ronald Reagan

Ronald Wilson Reagan was born on February 6, 1911, in Tampico, Illinois, the son of Jack and Nelle Reagan. Raised in a devoutly religious household with a strong emphasis on hard work and self-reliance, Reagan learned the values of thrift, discipline, and perseverance from an early age. After graduating from Eureka College in 1932, Reagan embarked on a career in entertainment, first as a radio announcer and later as a Hollywood actor.

Reagan's years in Hollywood provided him with a platform to hone his communication skills and develop a keen understanding of the power of storytelling and persuasion. Though he achieved moderate success as an actor, Reagan harbored political ambitions from an early age, inspired by the example of his father, who served as a local Democratic Party activist.

Reagan's first foray into politics came in the 1940s, when he became involved in the Screen Actors Guild (SAG), the labor union representing actors in the film industry. Elected president of SAG in 1947, Reagan quickly distinguished himself as a skilled negotiator and a passionate advocate for the rights of actors. His experiences in the world of labor politics would shape his views on the role of government and the importance of preserving individual freedom and economic opportunity.

In the 1950s, Reagan's political career took a conservative turn, as he became increasingly disillusioned with the growing influence of communism in Hollywood and the broader American society. A vocal critic of leftist ideology, Reagan emerged as a leading spokesperson for conservative causes, delivering stirring speeches and writing articles denouncing the perils of socialism and collectivism.

B. Presidential Campaigns: 1980 and 1984

Reagan's presidential ambitions took root in the 1960s, when he emerged as a prominent voice within the Republican Party, advocating for a return to conservative principles and a rejection of the perceived excesses of the liberal establishment. Though he initially hesitated to enter the political fray, Reagan's passion for public service and his concern for the direction of the country ultimately propelled him to seek higher office.

In 1966, Reagan made his first bid for political office, running for governor of California against incumbent Democrat Pat Brown. Running on a platform of fiscal conservatism and law and order, Reagan scored a decisive victory, capturing the governorship by a landslide margin. His two terms as governor would serve as a proving ground for his conservative agenda, as he implemented tax cuts, slashed government spending, and cracked down on crime, earning him widespread acclaim among conservatives nationwide.

Building on the success of his gubernatorial tenure, Reagan set his sights on the presidency, announcing his candidacy for the Republican nomination in 1976. Though he narrowly lost the nomination to incumbent President Gerald Ford, Reagan's strong showing in the primaries cemented his status as a rising star within the Republican Party and laid the groundwork for his eventual triumph in 1980.

The 1980 presidential campaign pitted Reagan against Democratic incumbent Jimmy Carter in a battle for the soul of America. Running on a platform of economic renewal, national defense, and a restoration of American values, Reagan captured the imagination of voters with his optimism, charisma, and unwavering commitment to his principles. Despite initial skepticism from the political establishment and the media, Reagan's message resonated with a broad cross-section of Americans, including disaffected Democrats and independent voters disillusioned by years of economic stagnation and foreign policy setbacks.

In November 1980, Reagan scored a decisive victory over Carter, winning 44 states and capturing nearly 51 percent of the popular vote. His landslide victory marked the beginning of a new era in American politics—a conservative revolution that would reshape the course of the nation's history for years to come.

Reagan's reelection campaign in 1984 was equally triumphant, as he won reelection in a historic landslide, carrying 49 states and earning over 58 percent of the popular vote—the largest electoral college victory in American history. His overwhelming victory reaffirmed the enduring appeal of his conservative vision and solidified his status as one of the most consequential presidents of the 20th century.

C. Reagan's Vision for America: Conservatism Takes Center Stage

At the heart of Ronald Reagan's vision for America was a deep-seated belief in the power of individual freedom, limited government, and free enterprise to unleash the nation's full potential and ensure a brighter future for all. Inspired by the principles of classical liberalism and the wisdom of America's founding fathers, Reagan sought to roll back the tide of big government and restore a sense of optimism and confidence in the American dream.

Central to Reagan's vision was his commitment to revitalizing the nation's economy through a program of tax cuts, deregulation, and fiscal discipline. Dubbed "Reaganomics," his economic policies aimed to unleash the creative energies of the free market and stimulate investment, innovation, and job creation. By slashing marginal tax rates, reducing regulatory burdens, and promoting sound monetary policies, Reagan succeeded in ushering in a new era of economic growth and prosperity, characterized by low inflation, rising productivity, and robust job growth.

Equally important to Reagan was his commitment to rebuilding America's military strength and restoring its position of leadership on the world stage. Recognizing the dangers posed by Soviet expansionism and the spread of communism, Reagan pursued a policy of peace through strength, bolstering defense spending, modernizing the armed forces, and deploying strategic defense initiatives such as the Strategic Defense Initiative (SDI), popularly known as "Star Wars." His unwavering resolve in confronting the Soviet Union and supporting freedom fighters around the world ultimately contributed to the collapse of the Soviet empire and the end of the Cold War.

Beyond his economic and foreign policy achievements, Reagan's presidency was characterized by a broader cultural and ideological shift—a renaissance of conservative values and traditions that permeated every aspect of American society. From his steadfast defense of traditional family values and his unwavering support for the sanctity of human life to his commitment to rolling back the tide of secularism and moral relativism, Reagan sought to restore a sense of moral clarity and purpose to the nation's public life.

In Reagan's America, patriotism was not a partisan sentiment but a unifying force that transcended political divides and inspired a renewed sense of pride and confidence in the American experiment. His belief in the inherent goodness of the American people and the enduring power of American ideals served as a beacon of hope for millions around the world, reminding us that, in the words of Reagan himself, "America's best days are yet to come."

Chapter III: Economic Revolution

Ronald Reagan's presidency ushered in a period of profound economic transformation, characterized by a bold agenda of tax cuts, deregulation, and free market policies aimed at revitalizing the nation's economy and restoring America's position as a global economic powerhouse. In this chapter, we will delve into the key components of Reaganomics—the economic philosophy that guided Reagan's approach to governance—and examine its impact on the American economy during the 1980s. From the implementation of supply-side economics to the deregulation of key industries, Reagan's economic policies laid the groundwork for a period of sustained growth and prosperity, but also set the stage for the economic challenges that would follow.

A. Reaganomics: Supply-Side Economics and Tax Cuts

At the heart of Reagan's economic agenda was the belief in the power of supply-side economics—the idea that reducing taxes and regulatory barriers would incentivize investment, spur economic growth, and ultimately generate more revenue for the government. Inspired by the theories of economists such as Arthur Laffer and Milton Friedman, Reagan sought to unleash the productive energies of the American people by freeing them from the burdens of excessive taxation and government intervention.

In 1981, Reagan signed into law the Economic Recovery Tax Act (ERTA), which represented the largest tax cut in American history at the time. The centerpiece of the ERTA was a dramatic reduction in marginal tax rates, with the top rate dropping from 70 percent to 50 percent and the bottom rate falling from 14 percent to 11 percent over a three-year period. These tax cuts were intended to stimulate investment, encourage entrepreneurship, and reward hard work, thereby unleashing a wave of economic growth and prosperity.

The effects of Reagan's tax cuts were immediate and profound. By putting more money back into the pockets of American taxpayers, Reagan's policies spurred consumer spending and investment, fueling a surge in economic activity and job creation. The stock market soared to new heights, business investment reached record levels, and unemployment fell to its lowest levels in decades. Inflation, which had plagued the economy throughout the 1970s, began to recede, paving the way for a period of sustained economic expansion.

But perhaps the most enduring legacy of Reaganomics was its impact on the federal budget deficit. Despite the optimistic projections of supply-side economists, Reagan's tax cuts failed to fully pay for themselves through increased economic growth, leading to a sharp increase in government borrowing and a ballooning of the national debt. Critics of Reaganomics argued that the tax cuts disproportionately benefited the wealthy and exacerbated income inequality, while also contributing to the widening budget deficit.

B. Deregulation and Free Market Policies

In addition to tax cuts, Reagan pursued a comprehensive agenda of deregulation aimed at reducing government interference in the economy and unleashing the forces of free enterprise. Reagan believed that excessive regulation stifled innovation, inhibited competition, and imposed unnecessary costs on businesses and consumers, thereby hampering economic growth and prosperity.

One of Reagan's first acts as president was to launch a sweeping campaign of deregulation across a wide range of industries, including transportation, energy, telecommunications, and finance. By lifting regulatory barriers and promoting competition, Reagan sought to create a more dynamic and flexible economy that could adapt to changing market conditions and unleash the creative energies of American entrepreneurs.

The effects of Reagan's deregulatory efforts were profound. In the airline industry, for example, the deregulation of the Civil Aeronautics Board (CAB) in 1978 led to a wave of new competition and innovation, resulting in lower fares, expanded routes, and increased consumer choice. Similarly, the deregulation of the telecommunications industry in the 1980s paved the way for the emergence of new technologies and services, such as cellular phones and cable television, that revolutionized the way Americans lived and worked.

Reagan's deregulatory agenda also extended to the financial sector, where he sought to dismantle many of the regulations that had been put in place during the Great Depression. The deregulation of savings and loan institutions, for example, led to a wave of risky lending and speculative investments that ultimately culminated in the savings and loan crisis of the late 1980s, which cost taxpayers billions of dollars in bailouts and regulatory interventions.

C. Impact on the Economy: Boom and Bust

The economic impact of Reagan's policies was profound, setting off a period of sustained growth and prosperity that came to be known as the "Reagan boom." By cutting taxes, reducing regulation, and promoting free market principles, Reagan unleashed the productive energies of the American people, leading to a surge in economic activity and job creation that transformed the nation's economy.

Gross domestic product (GDP) grew at an average annual rate of 3.5 percent during Reagan's presidency, outpacing the growth rates of the 1970s and laying the foundation for one of the longest peacetime expansions in American history. Unemployment fell from a peak of 10.8 percent in 1982 to a low of 5.3 percent by the time Reagan left office, as millions of Americans found jobs and rejoined the workforce.

But alongside the boom came the seeds of future economic challenges. Reagan's tax cuts, combined with increased defense spending and a reluctance to rein in entitlement programs, led to a sharp increase in government borrowing and a ballooning of the federal budget deficit. By the end of Reagan's presidency, the national debt had more than doubled, from $997 billion in 1981 to $2.85 trillion in 1989, raising concerns about the long-term sustainability of America's fiscal policies.

Moreover, the benefits of Reagan's economic policies were not evenly distributed. While the wealthy benefited disproportionately from the tax cuts, many working-class Americans saw their wages stagnate or decline in real terms, exacerbating income inequality and widening the gap between the haves and the have-nots. The savings and loan crisis, which erupted in the late 1980s, also underscored the dangers of deregulation and lax oversight, as hundreds of thrift institutions collapsed under the weight of bad loans and speculative investments.

In the end, Reagan's economic revolution left a mixed legacy—one of unparalleled growth and prosperity, but also of fiscal irresponsibility and structural imbalances that would come to haunt future generations. As America grappled with the challenges of the post-Reagan era, the lessons of Reaganomics would continue to shape the nation's economic policies and political debates for years to come.

Chapter IV: Foreign Policy Shifts

Ronald Reagan's presidency was marked by significant shifts in America's approach to foreign policy, as he sought to confront the challenges posed by the Soviet Union, advance the cause of freedom around the world, and restore America's position as a global superpower. In this chapter, we will explore the key elements of Reagan's foreign policy agenda, from his confrontations with the Soviet Union to his support for anti-communist movements abroad. We will also examine the Iran-Contra affair—a controversial episode that tested the limits of presidential power and shook the foundations of Reagan's presidency.

A. Cold War Dynamics: Reagan vs. the Soviet Union

At the heart of Reagan's foreign policy was his unwavering commitment to confronting the Soviet Union and rolling back the spread of communism around the world. Reagan viewed the Cold War as a struggle between good and evil, freedom and tyranny, and he believed that America had a moral obligation to stand up to Soviet aggression and support those who sought to throw off the yoke of communist oppression.

From the outset of his presidency, Reagan adopted a confrontational stance toward the Soviet Union, labeling it an "evil empire" and calling for a policy of "peace through strength." Determined to restore America's military superiority and project strength on the world stage, Reagan embarked on a massive military buildup, increasing defense spending by over 40 percent during his first term and launching ambitious programs such as the Strategic Defense Initiative (SDI), which aimed to develop a missile defense shield capable of protecting America from Soviet nuclear attacks.

Reagan's confrontational approach to the Soviet Union was met with fierce resistance from Moscow, as the two superpowers engaged in a series of escalating tensions and proxy conflicts around the world. From the deployment of Pershing II missiles in Western Europe to the support for anti-communist rebels in Afghanistan and Nicaragua, Reagan pursued a strategy of containment and rollback aimed at undermining Soviet influence and weakening its hold on its satellite states.

The culmination of Reagan's confrontational stance toward the Soviet Union came in 1987, with the signing of the Intermediate-Range Nuclear Forces (INF) Treaty—a landmark arms control agreement that banned the deployment of intermediate-range nuclear missiles in Europe. The INF Treaty marked a significant breakthrough in U.S.-Soviet relations, paving the way for further arms control agreements and ultimately contributing to the collapse of the Soviet empire.

B. Reagan Doctrine: Support for Anti-Communist Movements

Central to Reagan's foreign policy agenda was his embrace of the Reagan Doctrine—a strategy that sought to support anti-communist movements and resistance groups around the world in their struggle against Soviet-backed regimes and communist insurgencies. Reagan believed that by supporting freedom fighters and dissidents in countries such as Afghanistan, Nicaragua, and Angola, America could weaken the Soviet Union's grip on its satellite states and hasten the demise of communism.

In Afghanistan, Reagan provided extensive support to the mujahideen—the Afghan resistance fighters who were battling against the Soviet-backed government in Kabul. Through covert CIA operations and the provision of weapons, training, and financial assistance, Reagan sought to undermine the Soviet occupation and inflict a humiliating defeat on Moscow. The Soviet withdrawal from Afghanistan in 1989 was widely seen as a victory for the Reagan Doctrine and a testament to the power of American support for anti-communist movements.

Similarly, in Nicaragua, Reagan backed the Contras—the anti-communist rebels who were fighting to overthrow the leftist Sandinista government. Despite widespread criticism and controversy, Reagan remained steadfast in his support for the Contras, arguing that they were fighting for freedom and democracy against a regime that was aligned with America's enemies. The Iran-Contra affair, however, would tarnish Reagan's legacy and raise serious questions about the legality and morality of his support for the Contras.

C. Iran-Contra Affair: Controversy and Fallout

The Iran-Contra affair was perhaps the most controversial episode of Reagan's presidency—a scandal that rocked the foundations of his administration and called into question the integrity of America's foreign policy process. The affair involved two separate but interconnected operations: the sale of arms to Iran in exchange for the release of American hostages held by Iranian-backed militants in Lebanon, and the diversion of proceeds from those sales to fund the Contras in Nicaragua, in contravention of congressional restrictions.

The origins of the Iran-Contra affair can be traced back to Reagan's desire to secure the release of American hostages held in Lebanon by Iranian-backed militants. In an effort to open channels of communication with Tehran, Reagan authorized the sale of arms to Iran, despite the regime's status as a state sponsor of terrorism. The arms sales, which were conducted through intermediaries in Israel and the Middle East, were intended to demonstrate America's willingness to engage with Iran and seek a peaceful resolution to the hostage crisis.

Unbeknownst to Congress or the American public, however, a portion of the proceeds from the arms sales was diverted to fund the Contras in Nicaragua—a group that Congress had explicitly prohibited the Reagan administration from supporting through direct or indirect means. The diversion of funds, which was orchestrated by senior officials in the Reagan administration, including National Security Council (NSC) staff member Oliver North, was carried out in secret and without congressional oversight.

When news of the Iran-Contra affair broke in November 1986, it sent shockwaves through the Reagan administration and the nation at large. The revelation that senior officials in the Reagan administration had engaged in illegal and unauthorized activities raised serious questions about the integrity of America's foreign policy process and the extent of presidential power. Reagan, for his part, denied any knowledge of the diversion of funds and sought to distance himself from the scandal, insisting that he had not traded arms for hostages or violated the law.

Despite Reagan's efforts to contain the fallout from the Iran-Contra affair, the scandal tarnished his reputation and cast a shadow over the final years of his presidency. Several members of Reagan's administration, including Oliver North and National Security Adviser John Poindexter, were indicted and convicted on charges related to their involvement in the affair, though many of the convictions were later overturned on appeal. The affair also led to a series of congressional investigations and hearings, including the famous televised hearings conducted by the Senate Select Committee on Secret Military Assistance to Iran and the Nicaraguan Opposition, chaired by Senator Daniel Inouye.

In the end, the Iran-Contra affair served as a cautionary tale about the dangers of unchecked executive power and the need for robust oversight and accountability in America's foreign policy process. Though Reagan's legacy was tarnished by the scandal, his broader achievements in foreign policy—including the defeat of communism in the Soviet Union and the promotion of freedom and democracy around the world—would endure long after he left office.

Chapter V: Social and Cultural Transformation

Ronald Reagan's presidency coincided with a period of significant social and cultural transformation in America. From the rise of the Moral Majority and the Religious Right to the implementation of the War on Drugs and tough-on-crime policies, Reagan's administration left an indelible mark on the nation's social landscape. Additionally, the era saw a growing push for LGBTQ+ rights, which was met with conservative backlash. In this chapter, we will explore these themes in detail, examining their origins, impact, and legacy.

A. Moral Majority and the Religious Right

The Moral Majority and the Religious Right emerged as powerful political forces during the Reagan era, advocating for conservative values and mobilizing voters around issues such as abortion, school prayer, and traditional family values. Led by figures such as Jerry Falwell, Pat Robertson, and Phyllis Schlafly, these organizations sought to inject religious and moral considerations into the political arena, shaping public opinion and influencing policy decisions.

At the heart of the Moral Majority's agenda was a commitment to restoring America's moral fabric and upholding traditional Judeo-Christian values. Through grassroots organizing, media outreach, and political activism, the Moral Majority mobilized millions of evangelical Christians and social conservatives, galvanizing support for Reagan and other like-minded candidates who embraced their values.

One of the key battlegrounds for the Moral Majority and the Religious Right was the issue of abortion. Reagan, who was staunchly pro-life, sought to rally support for measures to restrict access to abortion and protect the rights of the unborn. His administration implemented policies such as the Mexico City Policy, which prohibited foreign aid from being used to fund organizations that provide or promote abortion overseas, and supported efforts to overturn Roe v. Wade, the landmark Supreme Court decision that legalized abortion nationwide.

In addition to their focus on social issues, the Moral Majority and the Religious Right also played a significant role in shaping America's foreign policy agenda, particularly in relation to Israel and the Middle East. Evangelical Christians, who viewed Israel as a key ally in the fight against communism and a fulfillment of biblical prophecy, lobbied for increased support for the Jewish state and played a pivotal role in shaping U.S. policy toward the region.

B. War on Drugs and Crime Policies

The Reagan era saw the implementation of aggressive policies aimed at combating drug abuse and violent crime, which had reached epidemic levels in many urban areas across America. Reagan, who declared a "War on Drugs" in 1982, sought to address the root causes of drug addiction and crime through a combination of law enforcement, prevention, and treatment initiatives.

One of the signature initiatives of Reagan's War on Drugs was the passage of the Anti-Drug Abuse Act of 1986, which imposed harsh mandatory minimum sentences for drug offenses and significantly expanded the federal government's role in drug enforcement. The law, which was championed by First Lady Nancy Reagan as part of her "Just Say No" anti-drug campaign, led to a dramatic increase in the incarceration rate for drug-related offenses, particularly among African American and Latino communities.

Reagan also implemented tough-on-crime policies aimed at cracking down on violent crime and gang activity. His administration advocated for stricter sentencing guidelines, expanded the use of capital punishment, and supported efforts to enhance law enforcement capabilities through increased funding and resources. The result was a sharp decline in crime rates during the latter half of the 1980s, as cities across America saw significant reductions in homicides, robberies, and other violent offenses.

However, the War on Drugs and tough-on-crime policies also had unintended consequences, including the disproportionate impact on minority communities and the erosion of civil liberties. Critics argued that Reagan's approach to drug policy focused too heavily on punishment and enforcement, while neglecting prevention and treatment initiatives. Moreover, the militarization of law enforcement and the use of tactics such as no-knock raids and asset forfeiture raised concerns about police brutality and overreach.

C. LGBTQ+ Rights and Conservative Backlash

The Reagan era saw a growing push for LGBTQ+ rights and recognition, as activists and advocates sought to challenge discrimination and secure equal rights under the law. However, this progress was met with fierce resistance from conservative groups and religious organizations, who viewed homosexuality as immoral and sought to roll back the gains made by the LGBTQ+ community.

One of the key battlegrounds for LGBTQ+ rights during the Reagan era was the issue of HIV/AIDS. The emergence of the AIDS epidemic in the early 1980s sparked a national conversation about public health and homosexuality, as thousands of Americans succumbed to the disease and communities grappled with fear, stigma, and misinformation. Reagan's response to the crisis was criticized by many activists and advocates, who accused his administration of being slow to act and indifferent to the plight of those affected by the disease.

In addition to the AIDS epidemic, Reagan's presidency also saw a series of legal battles and policy debates surrounding LGBTQ+ rights, including efforts to ban discrimination based on sexual orientation and gender identity, expand access to healthcare and social services for LGBTQ+ individuals, and repeal discriminatory laws and regulations.

Despite the progress made by the LGBTQ+ rights movement during the Reagan era, conservative backlash remained a formidable obstacle to full equality and acceptance. Conservative groups and religious organizations mobilized against efforts to advance LGBTQ+ rights, lobbying for measures to restrict same-sex marriage, block anti-discrimination laws, and promote so-called "family values" initiatives.

The legacy of the Reagan era on LGBTQ+ rights is complex and multifaceted. While Reagan himself did not openly champion LGBTQ+ rights and often clashed with activists and advocates on social issues, his presidency coincided with a period of growing awareness and visibility for the LGBTQ+ community. The battles fought and the victories won during the Reagan era laid the groundwork for the progress that would follow in the decades to come, as America continued its journey toward equality and inclusion for all.

Chapter VI: Supreme Court and Legal Legacy

The Supreme Court plays a crucial role in shaping the legal landscape of the United States, interpreting the Constitution, and adjudicating some of the most contentious issues facing the nation. During the Reagan era, the Supreme Court underwent significant changes, with the appointment of conservative justices and the rise of competing judicial philosophies. In this chapter, we will explore the impact of Reagan's appointments on the Supreme Court, examine the ideological shifts within the judiciary, and assess the lasting legacy of Reagan's Court on American law.

A. Appointments and Ideological Shifts

Ronald Reagan had a profound impact on the composition of the Supreme Court, making four appointments during his presidency: Sandra Day O'Connor, Antonin Scalia, Anthony Kennedy, and William Rehnquist (who was elevated to Chief Justice). These appointments represented a significant departure from the liberal-leaning Warren Court and marked the beginning of a conservative ascendancy on the bench.

1. Sandra Day O'Connor: In 1981, Reagan nominated Sandra Day O'Connor to the Supreme Court, making her the first woman to serve as a justice. O'Connor, a moderate conservative with a reputation for pragmatism and independence, would go on to play a pivotal role in many of the Court's landmark decisions, including cases involving abortion, affirmative action, and religious liberty.

2. Antonin Scalia: In 1986, Reagan appointed Antonin Scalia to the Supreme Court, solidifying the Court's conservative majority. Scalia, a staunch originalist and textualist, advocated for a strict interpretation of the Constitution and was known for his sharp wit and incisive writing style. Scalia's influence on the Court was profound, shaping its jurisprudence for decades to come.

3. Anthony Kennedy: Reagan's appointment of Anthony Kennedy in 1988 proved to be a pivotal moment for the Court. Kennedy, a centrist conservative with libertarian leanings, often served as the swing vote in closely divided cases, earning him the nickname "the Decider." Kennedy's jurisprudence reflected a

commitment to individual liberty and dignity, particularly in cases involving gay rights and abortion.

4. William Rehnquist: Reagan's elevation of William Rehnquist to Chief Justice in 1986 marked a significant shift in the Court's leadership. Rehnquist, a staunch conservative and originalist, sought to roll back the tide of judicial activism and promote a more restrained approach to constitutional interpretation. As Chief Justice, Rehnquist presided over a Court that became increasingly conservative in its outlook and jurisprudence.

Reagan's appointments to the Supreme Court reflected his commitment to reshaping the federal judiciary and advancing conservative principles through the courts. By appointing justices who shared his commitment to originalism, textualism, and judicial restraint, Reagan sought to leave a lasting imprint on the Court and ensure that his vision of America would endure for generations to come.

B. Judicial Activism vs. Originalism

The Reagan era saw a renewed debate over the proper role of the judiciary in American society, with competing visions of judicial activism and originalism vying for supremacy. Judicial activism, which advocates for an expansive interpretation of the Constitution and a willingness to overturn precedent in pursuit of social justice, had been a hallmark of the Warren Court and its liberal successors. Originalism, on the other hand, argues for a strict interpretation of the Constitution based on the original intent of the framers and a reluctance to depart from established precedent.

1. Judicial Activism: Critics of judicial activism argued that liberal judges had overstepped their bounds and usurped the role of the legislative branch by imposing their own policy preferences on the American people. They pointed to cases like Roe v. Wade, which legalized abortion nationwide, and Miranda v. Arizona, which established the right to remain silent during police interrogation, as examples of judicial overreach and activism.

2. Originalism: Advocates of originalism, including justices like Scalia and Rehnquist, argued that the Constitution should be interpreted according to its original meaning and the intent of the framers. They criticized the Warren Court for straying from the text and history of the Constitution and argued for a more

restrained approach to constitutional interpretation that deferred to the political branches and respected the democratic process.

The clash between judicial activism and originalism came to a head in many of the Supreme Court's most contentious cases, including those involving abortion, affirmative action, and the separation of powers. Reagan's appointments to the Court represented a victory for originalism and a repudiation of the liberal judicial activism of the Warren Court. However, the tension between these competing visions of the judiciary would continue to shape American law and politics for decades to come.

C. Legacy of Reagan's Court: Shaping American Law

The legacy of Reagan's Court is a complex and multifaceted one, marked by both triumphs and controversies. On the one hand, Reagan's appointments to the Supreme Court helped to solidify a conservative majority and advance a vision of America grounded in principles of limited government, individual liberty, and traditional values. Justices like Scalia and Rehnquist left an indelible mark on the Court, shaping its jurisprudence and influencing the direction of American law for generations to come.

On the other hand, Reagan's Court was not without its flaws and shortcomings. Critics argued that the Court's conservative majority often sided with powerful corporate interests at the expense of ordinary Americans, rolling back regulations and protections designed to safeguard workers, consumers, and the environment. The Court's decisions in cases like Citizens United v. FEC, which struck down limits on corporate campaign spending, and Shelby County v. Holder, which gutted key provisions of the Voting Rights Act, were seen as evidence of its pro-business and anti-democratic bias.

Moreover, Reagan's Court struggled to address some of the most pressing social and moral issues facing the nation, including abortion, affirmative action, and LGBTQ+ rights. While the Court made significant rulings in these areas, such as upholding restrictions on abortion in Webster v. Reproductive Health Services and striking down sodomy laws in Lawrence v. Texas, its decisions often reflected the deep divisions within American society and failed to provide definitive answers to these contentious questions.

In the end, the legacy of Reagan's Court is a contested one, with supporters hailing its commitment to originalism and judicial restraint and critics decrying its conservative activism and ideological bias. Whatever one's views on the Reagan Court, its impact on American law and society cannot be denied. Through its decisions and dissents, the Court shaped the contours of constitutional law, defined the scope of individual rights and freedoms, and left an enduring legacy that continues to shape the nation's legal and political landscape to this day.

Chapter VII: The Reagan Coalition

The Reagan Coalition was a diverse and formidable political alliance that played a crucial role in shaping American politics during the 1980s and beyond. Built on a foundation of conservative principles and populist appeal, the coalition brought together a broad array of interests and constituencies, from evangelical Christians and social conservatives to fiscal hawks and anti-communist hawks. In this chapter, we will explore the origins of the Reagan Coalition, examine the divisions within the Republican Party that emerged during Reagan's presidency, and assess the lasting impact of the coalition on subsequent elections and American politics.

A. Building a Political Movement: Alliance of Conservatives

Ronald Reagan's rise to power was fueled by a potent mix of conservative ideology, charismatic leadership, and grassroots organizing. From his early days as a Hollywood actor and spokesman for General Electric to his tenure as governor of California and ultimately president of the United States, Reagan cultivated a broad base of support among conservatives and libertarians who shared his vision of limited government, free markets, and traditional values.

At the heart of the Reagan Coalition was a commitment to rolling back the tide of liberalism and big government that had come to dominate American politics in the wake of the New Deal and the Great Society. Reagan tapped into widespread discontent with the direction of the country under Democratic rule, promising to restore America's greatness and usher in a new era of prosperity and freedom.

One of the key pillars of the Reagan Coalition was the Religious Right, which emerged as a powerful force in American politics during the 1980s. Evangelical Christians and social conservatives, galvanized by issues such as abortion, school prayer, and the perceived erosion of traditional values, rallied behind Reagan's candidacy and helped to mobilize millions of voters in support of his agenda.

Another crucial component of the Reagan Coalition was the conservative wing of the Republican Party, which had long been marginalized within the GOP establishment but found a champion in Reagan. Fiscal conservatives, anti-communist hawks, and proponents of limited government were drawn to Reagan's message of lower taxes, smaller government, and a strong national defense, seeing in him a leader who would advance their interests and ideals.

Reagan also forged alliances with other key constituencies, including blue-collar workers, suburbanites, and disaffected Democrats, who were attracted to his message of economic opportunity, individual responsibility, and national pride. By building a broad and diverse coalition of supporters, Reagan was able to transcend traditional party lines and appeal to a wide swath of the American electorate.

B. Divisions within the Republican Party

Despite Reagan's success in building a broad-based coalition of supporters, his presidency was not without its challenges and divisions within the Republican Party. Throughout his two terms in office, Reagan faced resistance from moderate Republicans and establishment figures who were skeptical of his conservative agenda and wary of his confrontational style.

One of the key flashpoints within the Republican Party during Reagan's presidency was the debate over fiscal policy and government spending. Reagan's ambitious agenda of tax cuts, defense buildup, and deregulation led to skyrocketing budget deficits and a ballooning national debt, which drew criticism from deficit hawks and fiscal conservatives who were concerned about the long-term implications of Reagan's fiscal policies.

Another source of division within the Republican Party was Reagan's approach to foreign policy and national security. While Reagan's confrontational stance toward the Soviet Union and support for anti-communist movements abroad won him praise from many conservatives, it also sparked opposition from moderate Republicans and proponents of détente who favored a more cautious and diplomatic approach to foreign affairs.

Reagan's handling of social issues, particularly abortion and LGBTQ+ rights, also exposed fault lines within the Republican Party. While Reagan himself was personally opposed to abortion and supportive of traditional family values, he faced pressure from moderate Republicans and pro-choice advocates to moderate his stance on social issues in order to broaden the party's appeal and appeal to independent voters.

Despite these divisions, Reagan's leadership and political acumen allowed him to navigate the internal conflicts within the Republican Party and maintain the cohesion of the Reagan Coalition throughout his presidency. By forging alliances with key constituencies and staying true to his conservative principles, Reagan was able to overcome opposition from within his own party and advance his agenda of limited government, free markets, and traditional values.

C. Impact on Subsequent Elections: Legacy of the Coalition

The Reagan Coalition left a lasting legacy on American politics, shaping the electoral landscape and influencing the direction of the Republican Party for decades to come. Reagan's landslide victories in the 1980 and 1984 presidential elections demonstrated the electoral potency of the coalition, as he won over large segments of the electorate and carried states that had long been Democratic strongholds.

Moreover, Reagan's success in building a broad-based coalition of supporters helped to redefine the political landscape and shift the center of gravity in American politics to the right. The Reagan Coalition laid the groundwork for the conservative resurgence that would sweep the country in the decades that followed, paving the way for the election of conservative presidents such as George H.W. Bush, George W. Bush, and Donald Trump.

However, the legacy of the Reagan Coalition is not without its controversies and contradictions. While Reagan's presidency was marked by significant achievements in areas such as tax reform, deregulation, and national defense, it also saw the emergence of deep divisions within American society and the Republican Party. The rise of the Religious Right and the ascendance of conservative ideology reshaped the political landscape, but also exacerbated social tensions and polarized the electorate along ideological lines.

Moreover, the Reagan Coalition's legacy is still hotly debated within the Republican Party, as competing factions vie for control of the party's future direction. The rise of the Tea Party movement and the election of populist leaders such as Donald Trump have exposed fault lines within the GOP and raised questions about the viability of Reagan's brand of conservatism in the 21st century.

In the end, the Reagan Coalition remains a potent symbol of the enduring power of conservative principles and grassroots organizing in American politics. While its legacy may be contested and its achievements may be debated, there is no denying the lasting impact of the coalition on subsequent elections and the trajectory of American history. As the Republican Party grapples with its identity and future direction, the lessons of the Reagan era continue to resonate and shape the contours of American politics for generations to come.

Chapter VIII: Social Welfare and Government Programs

The Reagan era was marked by a significant shift in the approach to social welfare and government programs, as Ronald Reagan and his administration pursued a policy agenda of cutbacks, austerity measures, and a reevaluation of the role of government in providing social services and safety nets. In this chapter, we will delve into the impact of Reagan's policies on social welfare programs, assess the consequences for vulnerable populations, and examine the broader debate over the role of government in addressing social and economic inequality.

A. Cutbacks and Austerity Measures

Ronald Reagan came into office with a mandate to shrink the size and scope of the federal government, and his administration wasted no time in pursuing an aggressive agenda of cutbacks and austerity measures aimed at reducing government spending and curbing the growth of social welfare programs. Reagan's philosophy of "supply-side economics" emphasized the importance of cutting taxes, deregulating the economy, and reducing government intervention in order to stimulate economic growth and unleash the power of the free market.

One of the first targets of Reagan's budget-cutting efforts was the social safety net established by the New Deal and the Great Society, which Reagan viewed as bloated, inefficient, and prone to abuse. Reagan sought to roll back the expansion of government initiated by his predecessors and return to a more limited conception of the role of government in providing for the needs of its citizens.

Reagan's budget proposals called for deep cuts to a wide range of social welfare programs, including Medicaid, food stamps, housing assistance, and education funding. His administration also sought to overhaul entitlement programs such as Social Security and Medicare, introducing measures to rein in spending and limit eligibility in order to reduce the burden on taxpayers and promote personal responsibility.

Reagan's budget-cutting efforts were met with fierce resistance from Democrats and advocacy groups, who argued that his policies would exacerbate poverty, inequality, and social dislocation. Critics accused Reagan of prioritizing the interests of the wealthy and powerful at the expense of the poor and vulnerable, and warned that his policies would lead to a dismantling of the social safety net and a widening of the gap between rich and poor.

B. Impact on Social Services and Safety Nets

The impact of Reagan's policies on social services and safety nets was profound and far-reaching, as millions of Americans saw their access to essential services and supports diminished or eliminated altogether. Cuts to programs such as Medicaid and food stamps left many low-income families struggling to make ends meet, while reductions in housing assistance and education funding forced others into homelessness or inadequate living conditions.

One of the most controversial aspects of Reagan's social welfare policies was his administration's response to the HIV/AIDS epidemic, which ravaged communities across America during the 1980s. Despite mounting evidence of the scale and severity of the crisis, Reagan's administration was slow to respond, cutting funding for public health programs and downplaying the urgency of the situation. As a result, thousands of Americans died needlessly from AIDS-related complications, while others struggled to access the care and support they desperately needed.

Reagan's policies also had a disproportionate impact on communities of color, exacerbating racial and economic disparities and deepening the divide between rich and poor. Cuts to social welfare programs disproportionately affected African American and Latino communities, which relied heavily on government assistance to meet their basic needs. Similarly, reductions in funding for education and job training programs limited opportunities for upward mobility and perpetuated cycles of poverty and inequality.

While Reagan's supporters argued that his policies were necessary to rein in government spending and promote economic growth, critics contended that the human cost of his austerity measures was too high to justify. They pointed to the millions of Americans who were left without access to adequate healthcare, housing, and education as evidence of the failure of Reagan's approach to social welfare and government programs.

C. Debate over the Role of Government: Limited vs. Expanded

At the heart of the debate over Reagan's social welfare policies was a fundamental disagreement over the role of government in addressing social and economic inequality. Reagan and his supporters argued for a more limited role for government, emphasizing the importance of individual initiative, personal responsibility, and free market solutions to social problems. They believed that government intervention in the economy and society was inherently inefficient and counterproductive, and that the best way to lift people out of poverty was to create the conditions for economic growth and job creation.

On the other side of the debate were those who advocated for an expanded role for government in providing social services and safety nets. They argued that Reagan's policies had failed to address the root causes of poverty and inequality, and that government had a moral obligation to ensure that all citizens had access to the basic necessities of life, such as healthcare, housing, and education. They called for increased investment in social welfare programs and a more proactive approach to addressing the structural barriers that perpetuated inequality and marginalization.

The debate over the role of government in addressing social welfare and economic inequality continues to resonate in American politics today, as policymakers grapple with the legacy of Reagan's policies and seek to chart a path forward that balances the competing demands of limited government and social justice. While Reagan's presidency was a watershed moment in the history of American conservatism and a turning point in the debate over the role of government, the issues he grappled with—poverty, inequality, and the social safety net—remain as relevant and pressing as ever, challenging policymakers and citizens alike to confront the complexities of a rapidly changing world.

Chapter IX: Environmental Policies and Conservation

The Reagan era witnessed significant changes in environmental policies and conservation efforts in the United States. Ronald Reagan and his administration pursued a deregulatory agenda, rolling back environmental regulations and promoting resource extraction. This chapter explores the impact of Reagan's policies on environmental protection, the debates over resource extraction versus preservation, and the lasting legacy on conservation efforts in the United States.

A. Rollbacks on Regulations

The Reagan administration came into office with a clear mandate to reduce government intervention in the economy, and this included scaling back environmental regulations perceived as burdensome to industry. Reagan's Environmental Protection Agency (EPA) Administrator, Anne Gorsuch Burford, implemented policies aimed at deregulating industry and streamlining environmental oversight. One of the most notable actions was the "regulatory relief" initiative, which aimed to reduce the regulatory burden on businesses by easing enforcement of environmental laws and regulations.

As part of its deregulatory agenda, the Reagan administration sought to weaken key environmental statutes, such as the Clean Air Act and the Clean Water Act, which had been passed in the 1970s to address pollution and protect public health and the environment. The administration pushed for amendments to these laws that would relax pollution standards, weaken enforcement mechanisms, and give industry more flexibility in complying with regulations.

The Reagan administration also sought to rein in the EPA's regulatory authority and limit its ability to impose new regulations on industry. This included efforts to cut the EPA's budget, reduce staffing levels, and dismantle key enforcement programs. The administration argued that these measures were necessary to spur economic growth and job creation, but critics accused Reagan of prioritizing the interests of polluters over the health and well-being of the American people.

B. Debates over Resource Extraction vs. Preservation

One of the central debates during the Reagan era was the balance between resource extraction and environmental preservation. Reagan and his supporters argued that excessive regulation and environmental activism were hindering economic development and stifling innovation. They advocated for opening up public lands and offshore areas to resource extraction, such as oil and gas drilling, mining, and logging, in order to stimulate economic growth and reduce dependence on foreign sources of energy.

Reagan's Secretary of the Interior, James Watt, was a staunch advocate for increased resource extraction on public lands and aggressively pursued policies to open up vast swaths of wilderness areas and national parks to development. Watt sought to expand oil and gas leasing, logging, and mineral extraction on federal lands, often in the face of opposition from environmental groups and conservationists.

The Reagan administration also sought to roll back environmental protections for sensitive ecosystems and endangered species, arguing that such protections were overly restrictive and impeded economic development. Reagan's policies led to a series of confrontations with environmental groups and conservationists, who mounted legal challenges and public protests in defense of America's natural heritage.

However, Reagan's push for increased resource extraction was not without its critics, who argued that his policies were shortsighted and environmentally destructive. They warned that opening up public lands to development would lead to irreversible damage to fragile ecosystems, threaten wildlife habitats, and exacerbate the impacts of climate change. They also raised concerns about the long-term consequences of pollution and environmental degradation on public health and the quality of life for future generations.

C. Legacy on Environmental Conservation Efforts

The Reagan administration's approach to environmental conservation had a lasting impact on conservation efforts in the United States. While Reagan's policies were criticized by many environmentalists and conservationists as harmful to the environment, they also galvanized public support for environmental protection and spurred a renewed commitment to conservation.

In response to Reagan's rollbacks on environmental regulations and resource extraction, environmental groups and conservationists mobilized to defend America's natural heritage and push back against efforts to weaken environmental protections. Grassroots organizations, such as the Sierra Club, the Wilderness Society, and the Natural Resources Defense Council, played a leading role in advocating for stronger environmental laws and regulations, mobilizing public support, and raising awareness about the importance of conservation.

Reagan's environmental policies also sparked a wave of activism and public engagement on environmental issues, as Americans became increasingly concerned about the impacts of pollution, habitat destruction, and climate change on their communities and the planet. The environmental movement grew in strength and influence during the Reagan era, organizing protests, lobbying lawmakers, and launching public education campaigns to raise awareness about environmental issues and promote sustainable solutions.

Despite the challenges posed by Reagan's deregulatory agenda, environmental conservation efforts made significant progress during his presidency. The establishment of new wilderness areas, national parks, and wildlife refuges, as well as the enactment of landmark legislation such as the Superfund program and the Coastal Zone Management Act, helped to protect and preserve millions of acres of land and water for future generations.

Moreover, Reagan's presidency served as a catalyst for a broader cultural shift towards environmental awareness and stewardship, inspiring a new generation of activists, scientists, and policymakers to prioritize conservation and sustainability in their work. The legacy of Reagan's environmental policies continues to shape the debate over environmental protection and conservation in the United States today, as policymakers grapple with the challenges of climate change, biodiversity loss, and environmental justice in the 21st century.

Chapter X: Media and Public Perception

The Reagan era was characterized by Ronald Reagan's exceptional communication skills, earning him the moniker "The Great Communicator." Reagan's ability to effectively communicate his message to the American people played a significant role in shaping his image and public perception. This chapter explores Reagan's communication prowess, the role of the media in shaping his image, and the myths and realities of the Reagan era.

A. Reagan's Communication Skills: The Great Communicator

Ronald Reagan was renowned for his exceptional communication skills, which became a defining feature of his political persona. With his folksy charm, persuasive rhetoric, and commanding presence, Reagan was able to connect with audiences across the political spectrum and convey his message with clarity and conviction.

Reagan's background as a Hollywood actor and radio personality gave him a natural flair for public speaking and storytelling, which he used to great effect on the campaign trail and as president. His speeches were often filled with memorable anecdotes, colorful language, and uplifting messages of American exceptionalism and optimism, which resonated with audiences and helped to cultivate a sense of national pride and unity.

One of Reagan's greatest strengths as a communicator was his ability to simplify complex issues and distill them into easily understandable terms. Whether he was discussing economics, foreign policy, or social issues, Reagan had a knack for breaking down complicated concepts into bite-sized soundbites that resonated with voters and reinforced his core message of limited government, individual freedom, and traditional values.

Reagan's communication skills were on full display during his famous televised addresses, such as his inaugural speeches, State of the Union addresses, and Oval Office addresses. These speeches were meticulously crafted to appeal to a broad audience and deliver a powerful message that captured the imagination of the American people.

B. Role of Media in Shaping Reagan's Image

The media played a crucial role in shaping Reagan's image and public perception during the Reagan era. Reagan's presidency coincided with the rise of cable news and the 24-hour news cycle, which brought politics into the living rooms of millions of Americans and made Reagan a ubiquitous presence in the media landscape.

Reagan was adept at using the media to his advantage, cultivating relationships with reporters and journalists, and leveraging his celebrity status to generate positive coverage. His administration carefully managed its interactions with the media, staging photo opportunities, crafting press releases, and controlling the narrative to ensure that Reagan's message was heard loud and clear.

Reagan's media strategy was based on the principles of image management and message discipline, which he had honed during his years in Hollywood and on the campaign trail. His administration worked tirelessly to shape Reagan's image as a strong and decisive leader, a champion of conservative values, and a defender of American interests at home and abroad.

However, Reagan's relationship with the media was not without its challenges. While he enjoyed widespread popularity and admiration from many quarters, Reagan also faced criticism and scrutiny from journalists and pundits who questioned his policies, his priorities, and his leadership style. His administration's handling of issues such as the Iran-Contra affair, the AIDS epidemic, and the environment drew sharp criticism from the media and eroded public confidence in his presidency.

C. Perception vs. Reality: Myths and Realities of the Reagan Era

The Reagan era was marked by a stark disconnect between perception and reality, as Reagan's image as "The Great Communicator" often overshadowed the complexities and contradictions of his presidency. While Reagan was celebrated as a transformative figure who restored America's confidence and prosperity, his presidency was also marked by controversy, conflict, and uncertainty.

One of the enduring myths of the Reagan era is the idea of Reagan as a fiscal conservative who championed small government and balanced budgets. While Reagan did advocate for tax cuts, deregulation, and reduced government spending, his administration also presided over a dramatic expansion of the federal deficit, which tripled during his time in office. Reagan's tax cuts, combined with increased defense spending and economic downturns, led to ballooning budget deficits and a legacy of debt that would shape the fiscal landscape for decades to come.

Another myth of the Reagan era is the idea of Reagan as a foreign policy mastermind who won the Cold War and restored America's standing in the world. While Reagan's confrontational stance toward the Soviet Union and his support for anti-communist movements undoubtedly played a role in hastening the collapse of the Soviet empire, his foreign policy record was also marked by missteps and controversies, such as the Iran-Contra affair and the invasion of Grenada.

Similarly, Reagan's record on social issues is often romanticized as a return to traditional values and moral clarity. While Reagan did champion conservative causes such as anti-abortion legislation and school prayer, his administration also faced criticism for its handling of issues such as HIV/AIDS, LGBTQ+ rights, and racial justice, which exposed deep divisions within American society and raised questions about the limits of Reagan's vision of America.

In the end, the Reagan era was a time of profound change and transformation in American politics and society. While Reagan's communication skills and media savvy helped to shape his image and define his presidency, the realities of his tenure in office were far more complex and nuanced than the myths and narratives that have come to define his legacy. As historians continue to reassess Reagan's presidency and its impact on America and the world, it is clear that the Reagan era remains a rich and contested chapter in the ongoing story of American democracy.

Chapter XI: Global Influence and Diplomacy

During the Reagan era, the United States wielded significant global influence and played a central role in shaping international affairs. Ronald Reagan's presidency was marked by his relationships with world leaders, the impact of Reaganomics on the global economy, and a mix of diplomatic successes and failures. This chapter examines these aspects of Reagan's global influence and diplomacy, highlighting the complexities and consequences of his foreign policy decisions.

A. Reagan's Relationships with World Leaders

Ronald Reagan's relationships with world leaders played a crucial role in shaping the course of international diplomacy during his presidency. From the Cold War standoff with the Soviet Union to the conflicts in the Middle East and Latin America, Reagan's personal rapport with foreign leaders often determined the outcome of key diplomatic negotiations and crises.

1. Mikhail Gorbachev: One of the defining features of Reagan's presidency was his relationship with Soviet leader Mikhail Gorbachev. Despite their ideological differences and the ongoing tensions between their two countries, Reagan and Gorbachev forged a personal bond based on mutual respect and a shared commitment to reducing nuclear weapons and ending the Cold War. The historic summits between Reagan and Gorbachev, including the Reykjavik Summit in 1986 and the Washington Summit in 1987, paved the way for landmark arms control agreements such as the Intermediate-Range Nuclear Forces Treaty (INF) and laid the groundwork for improved US-Soviet relations.

2. Margaret Thatcher: Reagan's relationship with British Prime Minister Margaret Thatcher was another key alliance that shaped his approach to foreign policy. Thatcher, a staunch conservative and ideological ally of Reagan, supported his aggressive stance toward the Soviet Union and his efforts to roll back communism in Eastern Europe. The close cooperation between Reagan and Thatcher, often referred to as the "special relationship," bolstered NATO's resolve and contributed to the success of Western efforts to contain Soviet expansionism.

3. Pope John Paul II: Reagan's relationship with Pope John Paul II, the charismatic leader of the Catholic Church, was instrumental in galvanizing opposition to communism in Eastern Europe and hastening the collapse of the Soviet empire. Reagan and the Pope shared a deep antipathy toward communism and a belief in the power of faith and freedom to overcome tyranny. The Pope's support for the Solidarity movement in Poland, combined with Reagan's diplomatic and military pressure on the Soviet Union, helped to undermine the legitimacy of the communist regime and embolden dissidents across the Eastern Bloc.

4. Ronald Reagan and World Leaders: In addition to his relationships with Gorbachev, Thatcher, and the Pope, Reagan cultivated ties with a wide range of world leaders, including West German Chancellor Helmut Kohl, French President François Mitterrand, and Japanese Prime Minister Yasuhiro Nakasone. Reagan's personal diplomacy and statesmanship helped to strengthen America's alliances and advance its interests on the global stage, earning him respect and admiration from leaders around the world.

B. Impact of Reaganomics on Global Economy

Reaganomics, the economic policies pursued by the Reagan administration, had a profound impact on the global economy during the 1980s. Reagan's policies, which emphasized tax cuts, deregulation, and free market principles, were intended to stimulate economic growth, reduce inflation, and create jobs. While Reaganomics had mixed results domestically, its impact on the global economy was far-reaching and complex.

1. Deregulation and Globalization: One of the hallmarks of Reaganomics was its emphasis on deregulation and free trade, which helped to spur economic globalization and integrate the world economy. Reagan's administration rolled back regulations on industries such as finance, telecommunications, and transportation, opening up new opportunities for investment and trade. The deregulation of financial markets, in particular, paved the way for the expansion of global capital flows and the rise of multinational corporations, transforming the landscape of the global economy.

2. Tax Cuts and Capital Flows: Reagan's tax cuts, which reduced marginal tax rates for individuals and corporations, incentivized investment and capital

formation, leading to an influx of foreign capital into the United States and other countries. The Reagan administration's policies created a favorable climate for business and entrepreneurship, attracting investment from around the world and fueling economic growth and innovation.

3. Impact on Developing Countries: While Reaganomics benefited the United States and other advanced economies, its impact on developing countries was more mixed. The deregulation of financial markets and the promotion of free trade led to increased capital flows and investment in developing countries, but also exposed them to the risks of financial instability and economic volatility. Moreover, Reagan's emphasis on market-oriented reforms and austerity measures contributed to widening income inequality and social unrest in many developing countries, exacerbating the challenges of poverty, unemployment, and social exclusion.

4. Reaganomics and the Global Economy: Overall, Reaganomics had a transformative impact on the global economy, accelerating the processes of economic globalization and financialization and reshaping the dynamics of international trade and investment. While Reagan's policies fueled economic growth and prosperity in the United States and other advanced economies, they also created new challenges and vulnerabilities, including income inequality, financial instability, and environmental degradation, that would shape the global economy in the decades to come.

C. Diplomatic Successes and Failures

The Reagan era was marked by a mix of diplomatic successes and failures, as Reagan pursued an ambitious agenda of promoting democracy, human rights, and free markets around the world. While Reagan's diplomacy helped to end the Cold War and advance America's interests on the global stage, it also faced setbacks and controversies that tested his leadership and resolve.

1. Successes in Ending the Cold War: Reagan's greatest diplomatic achievement was his role in ending the Cold War and bringing about the collapse of the Soviet Union. Through a combination of military buildup, economic pressure, and diplomatic engagement, Reagan and his administration compelled the Soviet leadership to recognize the futility of their efforts to compete with the United States and seek a peaceful resolution to the conflict. The signing of arms

control agreements such as the INF Treaty and the START Treaty, combined with Reagan's personal diplomacy with Gorbachev, laid the groundwork for the peaceful transition from the Cold War to a new era of cooperation and détente.

2. Failures in Latin America and the Middle East: Despite his success in ending the Cold War, Reagan's foreign policy faced significant challenges in other regions of the world, particularly Latin America and the Middle East. The Reagan administration's support for authoritarian regimes and counterinsurgency operations in countries such as El Salvador, Guatemala, and Nicaragua drew condemnation from human rights groups and fueled anti-American sentiment in the region. Similarly, Reagan's efforts to broker peace in the Middle East, including the ill-fated Iran-Contra affair and the bombing of Libya, were marred by controversy and criticism, undermining America's credibility and influence in the region.

3. Reagan's Legacy in Diplomacy: In the end, Reagan's legacy in diplomacy is a complex and contested one, shaped by both his successes and failures on the global stage. While Reagan's leadership played a crucial role in ending the Cold War and advancing America's interests, his administration's policies in Latin America and the Middle East left a legacy of conflict and instability that continues to reverberate today. As historians continue to reassess Reagan's foreign policy record and its impact on the world, it is clear that his presidency was a pivotal moment in the history of American diplomacy, with far-reaching consequences for the United States and its role in the world.

Chapter XII: Social Movements and Civil Rights

The Reagan era was a time of significant social change and activism, as various social movements fought for civil rights, equality, and justice. This chapter explores the impact of the Reagan era policies on the African American community, women's rights, and immigration, as well as the responses and challenges faced by these social movements during this period.

A. African American Community and Reagan Era Policies

The Reagan era was a challenging time for the African American community, as Reagan's policies often exacerbated existing inequalities and disparities. While Reagan enjoyed some support within the African American community, particularly among conservative African Americans who shared his values of individual responsibility and limited government, many African Americans felt marginalized and neglected by Reagan's administration.

1. Economic Policies: Reagan's economic policies, often referred to as Reaganomics, had a disproportionate impact on African Americans, who were already struggling with high rates of poverty and unemployment. Reagan's emphasis on tax cuts, deregulation, and trickle-down economics favored the wealthy and corporations at the expense of working-class Americans, exacerbating income inequality and widening the racial wealth gap.

2. War on Drugs: The Reagan administration's War on Drugs, launched in the early 1980s, had a devastating impact on African American communities, leading to mass incarceration, militarized policing, and the criminalization of drug addiction. The implementation of harsh sentencing laws, such as mandatory minimums and three-strikes laws, disproportionately targeted African Americans and contributed to the racial disparities in the criminal justice system that persist to this day.

3. Civil Rights: Despite Reagan's rhetoric of colorblindness and equal opportunity, his administration's record on civil rights was mixed at best. Reagan's opposition to affirmative action, voting rights protections, and other

civil rights measures drew criticism from civil rights leaders and activists, who accused him of rolling back the gains of the civil rights movement and undermining the progress towards racial equality.

B. Women's Rights and Feminist Responses

The Reagan era was a contentious time for women's rights and feminism, as Reagan's conservative policies clashed with the growing demands for gender equality and reproductive rights. While Reagan enjoyed support from some conservative women who shared his values of traditional family values and anti-abortion sentiments, many women's rights activists and feminists viewed his presidency as a threat to their hard-won gains.

1. Reproductive Rights: One of the most contentious issues during the Reagan era was abortion rights, as Reagan sought to overturn Roe v. Wade and restrict access to abortion services. Reagan's administration implemented policies such as the Mexico City Policy, which prohibited US funding for international family planning organizations that provided abortion services, and supported anti-abortion legislation at the state and federal levels.

2. Equal Pay and Workplace Discrimination: Despite Reagan's professed support for equal opportunity and meritocracy, his administration did little to address gender discrimination in the workplace or the gender pay gap. Reagan's opposition to affirmative action and workplace protections for women, combined with his emphasis on deregulation and free market principles, left many women feeling vulnerable and unprotected in the workplace.

3. Feminist Responses: In response to Reagan's conservative agenda, women's rights activists and feminists mobilized to defend reproductive rights, promote gender equality, and resist efforts to roll back the gains of the women's movement. Organizations such as the National Organization for Women (NOW), Planned Parenthood, and the Feminist Majority Foundation led grassroots campaigns, lobbied lawmakers, and organized protests to protect women's rights and advance feminist priorities.

C. Immigration and Border Policies

The Reagan era was a tumultuous time for immigration and border policies, as Reagan's administration implemented controversial measures to address the perceived threats of illegal immigration and border insecurity. While Reagan's policies sought to tighten border controls and crack down on undocumented immigrants, they also sparked controversy and criticism from immigrant rights advocates and civil liberties groups.

1. Immigration Reform and Control Act: One of the most significant immigration policies of the Reagan era was the Immigration Reform and Control Act (IRCA) of 1986, which sought to address the issue of illegal immigration through a combination of enforcement measures and amnesty provisions. The IRCA granted legal status to millions of undocumented immigrants who had been living in the United States since before 1982, while also increasing penalties for employers who hired undocumented workers and stepping up enforcement efforts along the US-Mexico border.

2. Border Security: Reagan's administration also ramped up efforts to secure the US-Mexico border, deploying more Border Patrol agents, increasing funding for border infrastructure, and implementing new surveillance technologies to detect and deter illegal crossings. However, these measures often had unintended consequences, such as increased migrant deaths along the border and human rights abuses by border enforcement agencies.

3. Challenges and Controversies: Reagan's immigration policies faced criticism from both sides of the political spectrum, with conservatives accusing him of granting amnesty to illegal immigrants and undermining border security, while liberals argued that his enforcement measures were overly harsh and punitive. The debate over immigration reform and border security would continue to shape US immigration policy in the decades that followed, with Reagan's legacy serving as a reminder of the complexities and challenges of managing immigration in a diverse and interconnected world.

In conclusion, the Reagan era was a time of significant social movements and civil rights activism, as various groups fought for equality, justice, and dignity in the face of conservative policies and challenges. While Reagan's presidency was marked by controversy and conflict on issues such as race, gender, and immigration, it also galvanized a new generation of activists and advocates who sought to build a more inclusive and equitable society for all Americans. As we continue to grapple with the legacy of the Reagan era, it is clear that the struggles for social justice and civil rights are ongoing, and that the lessons of the past must inform our efforts to create a better future for generations to come.

Chapter XIII: Legacy and Reassessment

As time passes and historical perspective deepens, the legacy of Ronald Reagan's presidency continues to be reassessed and debated. From his economic policies to his foreign relations strategies, Reagan's presidency left an indelible mark on American politics and society. This chapter delves into the evaluation of Reagan's presidency, explores its long-term impact on American politics and society, and examines contemporary views on the Reagan era.

A. Evaluating Reagan's Presidency: Successes and Failures

1. Economic Policy: Reagan's economic policies, commonly referred to as Reaganomics, are often cited as one of his most enduring legacies. The implementation of supply-side economics, characterized by tax cuts, deregulation, and a focus on reducing government spending, is credited with stimulating economic growth and curbing inflation. However, critics argue that Reaganomics exacerbated income inequality and led to a ballooning federal deficit, which would have long-term consequences for the US economy.

2. Foreign Policy: Reagan's approach to foreign policy, particularly his confrontational stance towards the Soviet Union, is widely regarded as one of his greatest successes. Through a combination of military build-up, diplomatic engagement, and strategic alliances, Reagan played a pivotal role in ending the Cold War and bringing about the collapse of the Soviet empire. However, his administration's support for anti-communist movements in Latin America and Africa, as well as the Iran-Contra affair, remain controversial aspects of his foreign policy legacy.

3. Social Policy: Reagan's social policies, including his stance on civil rights, women's rights, and immigration, continue to generate debate and controversy. While Reagan is celebrated by some as a champion of traditional values and limited government, others criticize his administration's record on issues such as racial equality, reproductive rights, and immigration reform. Reagan's approach to social welfare and government programs, characterized by cutbacks and

austerity measures, also remains a subject of contention among historians and policymakers.

B. Long-Term Impact on American Politics and Society

1. Conservative Movement: Reagan's presidency is widely credited with revitalizing the conservative movement in America and reshaping the ideological landscape of American politics. Reagan's emphasis on limited government, free markets, and traditional values galvanized a new generation of conservative activists and leaders, who would go on to dominate the Republican Party and shape its policy agenda for decades to come.

2. Polarization: The Reagan era is also associated with the rise of political polarization in America, as the country became increasingly divided along partisan lines. Reagan's conservative policies and rhetoric appealed to his base of supporters but alienated many progressives and moderates, contributing to a widening ideological divide that continues to define American politics today.

3. Economic Inequality: Reaganomics is often cited as a contributing factor to the widening income inequality and economic disparities that have characterized American society in recent decades. The Reagan era saw a dramatic shift in wealth and power towards the top earners, as tax cuts and deregulation favored the wealthy and exacerbated the gap between rich and poor. This legacy of Reaganomics continues to shape debates over economic policy and social justice in America.

C. Reactions and Revisions: Contemporary Views on the Reagan Era

1. Conservative Reassessment: Within the conservative movement, Reagan remains a revered figure and a symbol of the triumph of conservative principles. Conservatives view Reagan as a transformative leader who restored American greatness, revived the economy, and defeated communism. Reagan's legacy continues to inspire conservative politicians and activists, who seek to emulate his leadership style and policy agenda.

2. Progressive Critique: Among progressives and liberals, Reagan's presidency is often viewed less favorably, with critics highlighting his administration's record on civil rights, social welfare, and environmental protection. Progressives argue that Reagan's policies exacerbated inequality, undermined social progress, and left vulnerable populations behind. Reagan's legacy continues to be a source of controversy and debate within progressive circles, as activists and scholars seek to challenge the dominant narrative of his presidency.

3. Historical Reevaluation: In recent years, there has been a growing trend towards a more nuanced and critical assessment of Reagan's presidency among historians and scholars. While Reagan is still celebrated as a transformative leader who reshaped American politics and society, there is increasing recognition of the complexities and contradictions of his presidency. Historians are reassessing Reagan's record on issues such as race, gender, and economic inequality, and exploring the long-term consequences of his policies for American democracy and global politics.

In conclusion, the legacy of Ronald Reagan's presidency continues to be a subject of debate and discussion, as historians, policymakers, and the public grapple with its enduring impact on American politics and society. While Reagan is remembered as a transformative leader who revitalized conservatism and reshaped the global landscape, his presidency is also marked by controversies and contradictions that continue to shape the trajectory of American democracy. As we continue to reassess the Reagan era, it is essential to critically examine its successes and failures, its enduring legacies, and its lessons for the future of American governance.

Chapter XIV: Reagan's Later Years and Legacy

Following his presidency, Ronald Reagan's later years were marked by both personal challenges and continued public engagement. This chapter examines Reagan's post-presidential activities, his health struggles, and the legacy he left behind through the Reagan Legacy Foundation and various commemorative efforts.

A. Post-Presidential Activities and Health Issues

1. Retirement Years: After leaving office in January 1989, Ronald Reagan retired to his ranch in California, where he spent his time writing, giving speeches, and enjoying leisure activities such as horseback riding and spending time with his family. Despite stepping out of the political spotlight, Reagan remained a respected figure in American public life, sought after for his wisdom and perspective on national and international issues.

2. Alzheimer's Diagnosis: In 1994, Ronald Reagan was diagnosed with Alzheimer's disease, a progressive neurodegenerative condition that affects memory, cognition, and behavior. The diagnosis came as a shock to Reagan and his family, and marked the beginning of a long and difficult journey for the former president and his loved ones.

3. Public Awareness: Despite his diagnosis, Ronald Reagan continued to make public appearances and advocate for Alzheimer's awareness and research. He and his wife, Nancy Reagan, became outspoken advocates for Alzheimer's patients and their families, raising awareness about the disease and working to reduce the stigma surrounding it.

B. The Reagan Legacy Foundation and Commemorative Efforts

1. Creation of the Reagan Legacy Foundation: In 1997, Ronald and Nancy Reagan established the Ronald Reagan Presidential Foundation and Institute, known as the Reagan Legacy Foundation, to preserve and promote the legacy of the Reagan presidency. The foundation is dedicated to advancing the principles

and values that Reagan championed, including limited government, free markets, and individual liberty.

2. Reagan Presidential Library: The Reagan Legacy Foundation oversees the Ronald Reagan Presidential Library and Museum, located in Simi Valley, California. The library houses the official records and artifacts of the Reagan presidency, as well as exhibits and educational programs that explore Reagan's life and legacy. It serves as a tribute to Reagan's leadership and a place of learning and inspiration for future generations.

3. Educational Initiatives: In addition to preserving Reagan's legacy, the Reagan Legacy Foundation sponsors educational initiatives and programs aimed at promoting civic engagement and leadership development among young people. These initiatives include scholarships, internships, and fellowships that provide students with opportunities to learn about Reagan's presidency and its impact on American history and politics.

C. Remembering Reagan: Tributes and Memorials

1. National Tributes: In the years following his death in 2004, Ronald Reagan was honored with numerous tributes and memorials across the United States. These included the renaming of landmarks, buildings, and highways in his honor, as well as the creation of statues, monuments, and memorials commemorating his life and legacy. Reagan's birthday, February 6th, is celebrated as Ronald Reagan Day in several states, and his legacy is remembered and honored through ceremonies, events, and educational programs.

2. International Recognition: Ronald Reagan's legacy extends beyond the borders of the United States, with numerous countries around the world paying tribute to his leadership and contributions to global politics. In Eastern Europe, Reagan is revered as a hero for his role in ending the Cold War and defeating communism, while in Western Europe and other parts of the world, he is remembered as a symbol of American strength and resolve.

3. Cultural Impact: Ronald Reagan's influence extends beyond politics to popular culture, where he is often portrayed in films, television shows, and works of literature as a larger-than-life figure who shaped the course of history. Reagan's speeches, quotes, and catchphrases have become iconic symbols of American conservatism and continue to resonate with audiences around the world.

In conclusion, Ronald Reagan's later years were marked by both personal challenges and continued public engagement, as he and his wife, Nancy Reagan, worked to preserve and promote his legacy through the Reagan Legacy Foundation and various commemorative efforts. Reagan's impact on American politics, society, and culture remains enduring, as his principles and values continue to shape the national discourse and inspire future generations of leaders.

Chapter XV: Conclusion

The Reagan era, spanning from 1981 to 1989, left an indelible mark on American politics, society, and culture. Ronald Reagan's presidency was marked by transformative policies, seismic shifts in foreign relations, and enduring ideological divides. As we conclude our examination of the Reagan era, we reflect on its enduring legacy, the lessons learned, and the challenges ahead for American democracy.

A. The Enduring Legacy of the Reagan Era

1. Conservative Resurgence: The Reagan era is often credited with revitalizing the conservative movement in America and reshaping the ideological landscape of American politics. Reagan's emphasis on limited government, free markets, and traditional values galvanized a new generation of conservative activists and leaders, who would go on to dominate the Republican Party and shape its policy agenda for decades to come. The legacy of Reaganism continues to influence conservative politics in the United States, shaping debates over economic policy, social issues, and the role of government in society.

2. Economic Transformation: Reaganomics, the economic policies pursued by the Reagan administration, had a profound impact on the American economy and the global economic order. Reagan's emphasis on tax cuts, deregulation, and free market principles helped to stimulate economic growth and curb inflation, but also exacerbated income inequality and led to a ballooning federal deficit. The legacy of Reaganomics continues to shape debates over economic policy and social justice in America, as policymakers grapple with the challenges of promoting prosperity while ensuring equity and opportunity for all Americans.

3. Foreign Policy Shifts: The Reagan era was characterized by a dramatic shift in American foreign policy, marked by Reagan's confrontational stance towards the Soviet Union and his efforts to roll back communism around the world. Through a combination of military build-up, diplomatic engagement, and strategic alliances, Reagan played a pivotal role in ending the Cold War and bringing about the collapse of the Soviet empire. The legacy of Reagan's foreign policy continues to shape America's approach to global affairs, as policymakers

navigate the complexities of great power competition, regional conflicts, and emerging threats to international security.

B. Lessons Learned and Challenges Ahead

1. Bipartisanship and Compromise: One of the enduring lessons of the Reagan era is the importance of bipartisanship and compromise in American politics. Despite their ideological differences, Reagan and Democratic leaders in Congress were able to find common ground on key issues such as tax reform, Social Security, and immigration. The spirit of bipartisanship that characterized the Reagan era stands in stark contrast to the partisan gridlock and polarization that plague contemporary American politics, underscoring the need for leaders who are willing to reach across the aisle and work together to address the challenges facing the nation.

2. Economic Equity and Social Justice: The Reagan era also highlighted the need to address the underlying causes of economic inequality and social injustice in America. While Reaganomics helped to spur economic growth and prosperity for some, it also widened the gap between rich and poor and left many Americans behind. The legacy of the Reagan era serves as a reminder of the importance of promoting economic equity and social justice, ensuring that all Americans have access to opportunities for success and upward mobility.

3. Democratic Institutions and Norms: The Reagan era underscored the importance of protecting and defending America's democratic institutions and norms. Despite his criticisms of government and calls for limited government intervention, Reagan respected the rule of law and the constitutional principles that underpin American democracy. In an era of rising authoritarianism and democratic backsliding, the legacy of Reagan reminds us of the fragility of democracy and the need to safeguard its institutions and values.

C. Reaganism in the 21st Century: Continuity and Change

1. Policy Continuity: While the Reagan era may seem like a distant memory, many of the policy debates and ideological divides that defined Reagan's presidency continue to shape American politics in the 21st century. The legacy

of Reaganism can be seen in debates over tax policy, healthcare reform, immigration, and foreign policy, as policymakers grapple with the enduring legacy of Reagan's presidency and its impact on American society.

2. Changing Demographics and Values: At the same time, America has undergone significant demographic and cultural changes since the Reagan era, challenging the traditional pillars of Reaganism and reshaping the political landscape. The growing diversity of the American population, the rise of social movements such as Black Lives Matter and #MeToo, and the increasing polarization of American society are all reshaping the contours of American politics and forcing policymakers to confront new challenges and priorities.

3. Reevaluation and Reassessment: As we look back on the Reagan era, it is essential to engage in a process of reevaluation and reassessment, critically examining Reagan's policies, his legacy, and his impact on American democracy. While Reagan is celebrated as a transformative leader who reshaped American politics and society, his presidency was also marked by controversies and contradictions that continue to shape the trajectory of American governance. By learning from the successes and failures of the Reagan era, we can chart a path forward towards a more inclusive, equitable, and democratic future for all Americans.

In conclusion, the Reagan era remains a pivotal moment in American history, with a legacy that continues to shape American politics, society, and culture. As we reflect on the enduring impact of Reaganism and its lessons for the present and future, we must strive to build upon the successes of the Reagan era while addressing its shortcomings and challenges. By engaging in honest dialogue, promoting bipartisan cooperation, and upholding democratic values, we can build a more prosperous, just, and inclusive society for generations to come.

Don't miss out!

Visit the website below and you can sign up to receive emails whenever Michael Johnson publishes a new book. There's no charge and no obligation.

https://books2read.com/r/B-A-OREFB-ZMXAD

BOOKS 2 READ

Connecting independent readers to independent writers.

Did you love *The Reagan Era*? Then you should read *The Civil Rights Movement*[1] by Michael Johnson!

Delve into the dynamic history of the Civil Rights Movement with this comprehensive guide. From its origins in Reconstruction to contemporary activism, explore pivotal moments, key figures, and enduring legacies. Chapters cover landmark events like Brown v. Board of Education and the March on Washington, as well as the evolution of strategies, from nonviolent resistance to Black Power. Reflect on intersectionality, voting rights, and ongoing challenges, offering insights into the past, present, and future of the fight for equality. A vital resource for understanding the complexities and significance of civil rights in America.

---

1. https://books2read.com/u/38JDgZ

2. https://books2read.com/u/38JDgZ

About the Author

Michael Johnson is a distinguished historian specializing in American history. With a degree in History from Harvard University, Johnson's work delves into pivotal moments, figures, and themes shaping the United States. He has authored numerous acclaimed books, offering insightful perspectives and engaging narratives. Johnson's commitment to meticulous scholarship and compelling storytelling has earned him widespread acclaim in the field. Passionate about sharing his expertise, he frequently engages in lectures and public events to foster a deeper appreciation for America's past.